deer hoof on river cobbles

deer
hoof
on
river
cobbles

· p o e m s ·

Walker Abel

WAYFARER BOOKS
BERKSHIRE MOUNTAINS, MASS.

WWW.WAYFARERBOOKS.ORG

Cover Design and Interior Design by Leslie M. Browning
Interior Opening Image: © Tomasz Filipek
Interior Image: © Sagar kulkarni
Cover Image: © Juliane Liebermann
First Edition Trade Paperback 978-1-956368-11-6

10 9 8 7 6 5 4 3 2 1

Wayfarer Books is committed to ecological stewardship. We greatly value the natural environment and invest in environmental conservation. For each book purchased in our online store we plant one tree.

FOR WILLOW

because the depth of your feeling
for the beauty
of earth, life, and love
has been the rain
watering the terrain of my poetry.

Contents

xi   Preface: Contemplations for Reading These Poems

1   Brambled Banks of Rivers

13   Fringes of Auburn and Gold

25   No Softer Bed

39   Small Bird of Particulars

51   Upstream in My Chest

65   Tangled Art of Aspen Leaf with Wind

77   Chipped as Mottled Sky

89   Last Utterance of the Maples

105   Addendum: Poetry, Qigong,
        and the Expansive Moment

Acknowledgments

About the Author

About the Press

preface

Contemplations for Reading These Poems

1.

Like listening to instrumental music
or gazing at abstract or impressionistic art
can I notice what effects come to me
rather than pushing
to figure out what the poem means?

2.

If each poem is its own being
like a plant or animal
can I let the presence and the gestures of that being
have their place in the world—
something arisen out of Mystery
representative not of a life
but of Life?

3.

A novelist must speak
from a multitude of voices.
Myth, dream, fairy tale
spin among many archetypes.
Rather than a history that has already happened
can I relate to each poem as a potentiality
of person, place, event

empathetically step into it
as one configuration of elements
one cloud-shape out of an endless sky?

4.
If poems are an expression of life
and if life is an expression of complementarities
can I be open to discovering
in the tones, images, and intimations of the poems
what I also discover in life
which is the swirling unfathomable intimacy of:
infinity/eternity
space/time
yin/yang
Earth/Heaven
form/emptiness
presence/absence
here/now
known/knower
matter/consciousness
beloved/lover
?

brambled

banks

of

rivers

———

Everywhere petals are flying
And Spring is fading. Ten thousand
Atoms of sorrow whirl away
In the wind. I will watch the last
Flowers as they fade....

—TU FU

Heaven and Earth are like two handles of a bellows
that push together and pull apart,
forever creating Life.

—LAO TZU, TRANS. TIM FREKE

Oblivion and Communion

The mountain looms over me its reverberations of silence.
And forest air is a sea taciturn as ground.

Yet high overhead, the relentless sweep
of a thousand clouds to follow or become.

I am forgetting how to breathe like the bear
in the winter of its snow-dusted rest.

The smallest mouse under heaps of bark and duff
rolls in its hands the seed of the world.

Then out of the gifting lips of eternity
this brief music—

two branches
breeze-blown against each other.

Drifters Along the Coast

Sadness of lovers and dying ones, of wanderers
who build castaway shelters by the sea
songs that count on nothing further than the night.

How the waves quieted as the tide went out
faces fragile with ember glow, and a world of mist
softening the salt dunes of touch.

Driftwood is bound by the ocean that bears it.
Oh that dark green water spinning down and down
that wreckage that never reaches bottom.

Reprieve

Some mornings the lake is so still
birdsong ricochets like glimmers of light

and brown-skinned rocks plump as manatees
rise slow from depths of jade-thick waters

as sailors might see mermaids—
a salvation breaking long-haired
from the very water that trapped them.

Dawn

On morning river rocks, a patina of silver frost
becomes wet sheen, then wisps of vapor.

Starlit hands alchemically adroit
had assembled ornate fabric—

the color of pearly everlasting
that might be hung from rafters—

the color of wedding dress
draped by window.

When fire in stove is nothing but ember
the bride rises to go outside.

She sees river leaving the room of night
and closing the door so softly

no dream is broke.

The Unborn

Before the river of morning
has carried its pebbles far
there's a stillness like trout
poised in green current of trees.

Tail sways with no motion.
Eye— a colorless hollow
that clouds pass through.

And nothing held the moon last night
were it not that empty mouth
that soft cavern

before the gills open like red flame
a wound in water
then close again
bloodless, healed.

Intimacy

He heard the singing even before he woke.
As in light rain, when water gathers on leaf
there's a tremble, there's the edge of dropping.

It's a fall toward earth, though longings
still press to wet face of sky.

Now everywhere is home.
The wagon rolls with its high wheels
and casts a humped shadow
along brambled banks of rivers
along dirt paths smelling of blankets and farewells.

Raising head and looking about
he is in mountains. It's autumn.
Tendrils mute as light
wrap him like another voice
into the song of yellow aspens.

Plea

White clouds wing high up—
some migration true to course.

And I remember now
what I am destined to forget again.

Dry grass falls
under belly of pressing cloud—
a frayed letter feathered along.

If you can hear me
speak in wind

say how leaves let go
how stone leans into snow.

fringes

of

auburn

and gold

She is braiding the waters of air into the plaited manes
Of happy colts,
They canter, without making a sound, along the shores
Of melting snow.

–JAMES WRIGHT

And then I feel the sun itself
as it blazes over the hills,
like a million flowers on fire—
clearly I'm not needed,
yet I feel myself turning
into something of inexplicable value.

–MARY OLIVER

Spell

Once there were dragonflies above the river
and by some murmur in the marrow

I knew the dream was pledge
you placed for me to find.

They almost woke me— their blue bodies
the river shimmering in steady light.

But I slept a while longer.
Slept in water, slept in web

slept with sense of something more
to the weave than I could remember.

Yes, something more
in the blue weave to remember.

Auburn and Gold

Deer in damp morning move across meadow grass.
You whispered me that as I woke and later
we saw bent blades, path of silver droplets.

By then ocean had first whitecaps—
winds of day rising to disperse memory of moon.

Days and nights are nothing but expanse of open sail
cupping a force that shepherds them headlong
to some island of shipwrecks, fog-cries of gulls.

Now I'm remembering the deer again
how we saw sun fringe their ears in auburn and gold.

The ocean, the ocean. Everywhere I look
shimmering spinnakers hover at the lip of horizon.

Manifesto

One more bold taste you tell me
then spin on toe
hurl the drained goblet
to shatter in stone hearth.

You have shed clothing like silver trails of comets.
They hang about the room the way nights always do
full of mountains and feathers and coastlines of pebbled shell.

I drink darkness the white moon passes through.
Everything's here, even the old arched arbor
that leads down flagstone steps to bird bath.

Even the droplets like planets thrown outwards
from shimmying sparrow.

All things dusted now in that light.

Closer than skin
you are wind through endless grasses.

Of Fair Tales

Tonight I am sleepless as the leaves
that lie sleepless on the ground.

Tonight I hear stories that like stars
whisper a place always true.

Once she was near me—
a breath in my breath.
We ate watercress green from streamside.

Once of wild horses, a small herd
and a white stallion no one could near.
Stout-legged his hooves and the sky.

Once on mountainsides, prayers
could be placed inside feathers
then earth-tied to destiny of clouds.

Arriving to shore, firelight falls first
on her skirt of shells, then on her hair.
Some singing passes beyond horizon

and each time out over the ocean
the old canoes rough-hewn
cut clean ripples above the depth.

Deer Hoof, River Cobbles

She said that people once
danced with anklets of deer hoof
that out on river terrace even now
their steps pool up with moonlight.

Behind every tree, she said
an unseen column of space.
That after sticks are gathered
beauty burns with fugitive heat.

Then autumn, and he remembers again
the formations of geese, their calls
first faint, but finally high up
the flicker of light off wings.

It seemed the breath of her being
was like that, a migration
he might step into, be lost with
above geese, above clouds

fallen in with a herd of stars
traipsing the dark turf
that undergirds galaxies

exhaled into the endless hollows
before alighting again
alone, moonlit, a deer hoof
dancing on river cobbles.

To Die For

Followed a bird four days through desert.
Do you know how it is to run like that?

We slept on steep ledges and started
each morning with song. When sunsets came
I knew the stars would nest us.

She molted with colors
of striate mountains, preened
in sinews of pinyon pine.

Woke today beneath branches
that had rained themselves bare when she flew.
First light sheened off silent stones.

By stripping time this spare
the naked moment
hatches out of thinnest air.

Lifting Anchor

Once known and unknown blended like water in a stream
and I was left on the bank of a world
where ferns waver between frond and wing.

Sing a song to the moon, and it boomerangs back
with a sweetness of shadow. To the sun
and the light of years falls like a single veined leaf.

Calling and calling, the body of love
is alive with animals and rivers
with distances that burst when horizons touch.

Forever you want me to say but never is just as true
like lifting anchor from a sea that drifts
in a darkness before first phosphorescence of you.

no
softer
bed

———————

The days are stacked against
what we think we are.
After a month of interior weeping
it occurred to me that in times like these
I have nothing to fall back on
except the sun and moon and earth.

—JIM HARRISON

The fate of the poor shepherd,
who, blinded and lost in the snow-storm,
perishes in a drift within a few feet of his cottage door,
is an emblem of the state of man.
On the brink of the waters of life and truth,
we are miserably dying.

—RALPH WALDO EMERSON

Moon Behind Freezing Clouds

Cold night by Yolla Bolly pond
rain turning to snow. The frogs
though neck-deep in that water, sing.

Upon arrival, a bear runs
from the meadow like Ursa Major
four points focused and surging ahead.

This life is not about happiness—
it's about trouble.
The trouble of orienting

the trouble of an ongoing song
gutty and tremulous
through the throes of season.

Portage

Once I did not know where I was
except that it was close to where I wanted to be

but close is not so different from far
when night is falling.

I shouldered canoe, was ready
for ease of water
but lake I could not find—

only fallen trees snapped and tangled
by some former fist of wind

and so I went round to get forward
and round further till forward
was as lost to me as backward.

Pressed by weight and weariness
I wondered what had me now in hand
and why I was handed this knot

and all the while the lake I sought
had not moved from where it was

though light faded from its shores
and stars in innocence
began to skitter its surface.

Alone

I cannot find the wind
that carries blessing into reach.

Small fires light the hills
but darkness rules the collapsed fields.

It was yesterday. Or the month before.
I was alone in some recess
lit by failing stars.

Was it dream or vision
those etchings of dieties
so fervent on frosted rock?

No one falls any farther
than their own doom.

Moss

If your boat breaks hull against rock
you can still flail in water
like cormorant on crippled wing.

Beyond outermost bastion of stone
waves take a blue turn.
You can follow into mending.

A bank of fog heads shoreward
toward forest of alder and fir.
There's no softer bed than moss.

Grief and Joy

Returning now, as all things come back—
the bird is folded into egg
swims again in yellow yolk.

Winds circle to source
and rivers swallow the head
of their own valley.

Returning now to my grief
returning now to my joy
mountains tuck wings

dive into sea
then rise cloud-feathered
out of that shell of nothing.

In all this commotion, let's not
forget the crows, the cormorants

how they lift from offshore rock
like black flags of risen earth.

Long Trail

Beyond the wind that now scrapes rock on furthest ridge
I'll find the sleep I needed yesterday.

There were markings once, a cloud-shift cipher.
Then drums and firelight ritual, a hand

tore open beehive-flame
and I tasted honey as I fell.

At every waterfall I bare my body
even freshets reached on glacier snow.

That cold, you said it's full of mirrors
and staunch as fire that scours a wound.

Prayer

All yearning
is to leap after you like deer.

And all burden:
to lose you in steep terrain
in crags or fissures of rock.

—

Grant me green days of forgiveness.
Let me go loosely again
like leaves on mirror of water.

Dawn and dusk: may their winds
sweep me wingless and welcome
at home in the vastness of your ways.

—

I'm lost under trees
that press all ardor out of air.

Marooned for months—
marooned in stunted worlds I make.

—

Later, the moon has waxed
or the moon has waned.
I wake at your camp.
Two bear are wandering the slope.

They watch casually
as though I'm always
being born in your arms.

small
bird
of
particulars

I am he that walks with the tender and growing night,
I call to the earth and sea half-held by the night.
Press close bare-bosom'd night— press magnetic nourishing night!
Night of south winds— night of the large few stars!
Still nodding night close — mad naked summer night.

– WALT WHITMAN

The actual goal of life however,
from a panpsychist point of view,
is not release from suffering, not salvation nor redemption,
but potentiation, the sizzling charge that accrues
from contact with the live subjectivity of all that is.

–FREYA MATHEWS

Everyday Magic

The waves, in nearing shore, rise
and in their rising, push

and the cupping wings of pelicans
catch the surge of that push

heavy bills and bodies
magically made buoyant.

With feathertips unflinching
a mere blade above the blue

the birds sail between beats
longer than seems lawful—

suspense hangs, breaths hold—

till at last they nonchalantly
lift and tilt over the curling crest

and the woman centuries ago
sawed in half, steps out whole.

Curtain of Rain

Feathered glints of day and night
small bird of particulars
you land with more weight
than water's surface bears
thus am I lifted, thrown
into lattices of depth and height.

Aspirations of the sky
defer to space and blue
reflected in compactness of your eye.

Leave me nothing when I end
but tracks of you in mud and sand
and just before the curtain of rain
let me hear that song of yours
that brings to joy its pain.

Seasons

Once, it was first rain of autumn.
Smell of wet earth rose
from having lain long dormant
and drifted with sound of surf.

It was raining, and it was dark
there was little wind over sea
and smell of wet earth
light-footed as a ghost
tried to remember itself out of the past
a relative returned, wrapped in old shawl
walking now under trees, out into soggy meadows
where that very day
turkeys had ambled among still-brittle stalks.

The dry smell gone now
like whales on long journey
how something so large can arch its back
dip below surface of seasons, gone into falling water
gray clouds, rolling distances of sea.

And tomorrow in early light
along the length of weed-strewn beach
gulls spectral in fog will search out stranded starfish
tilt head to gulp them whole
and what for a time had crawled on ocean floor
will now take a turn in the sky.

The Unchanging

It was then as though the world
were made of light

how it flared
in white spray of waves over rock

burned even in the blue of water
while sky burned blue as well

but lighter, as though thinned with itself
and spread so broadly as to be dimensionless

made to merge with the transparent light
that held still in its own being

not moved by forceful wind
not blocked by clouds or wings of gull

a light undiminished, full and present
in even the darkest shadow

here beneath the willows
ruffling along riverside.

Desert Shade

To fall in
like a voice
into nothing it can speak—

so cool
the hot sentence of the self
stutters into silence—

and the stranded word
finds itself unwritten
in the stillness before syllables.

No Boundary

A broad meadow—
slopes and terraces, dips and undulations.

Privacy can turn inside out
world can enfold within

as the blooming redbud's tune of color
is both its own and the earth's

as rattle in hand, buoyed by two legs
the place flows by as song.

upstream

in

my

chest

...the rest of my days I spend
wandering: wondering
what, anyway,
was that sticky infusion, that rank flavor of blood, that
poetry by which I lived?
—*GALWAY KINNELL*

As I see my soul reflected in Nature,
As I see through a mist,
One with inexpressible completeness, sanity, beauty,
See the bent head and arms folded
over the breast, the Female I see.
—*WALT WHITMAN*

Autumnal

If she can't say it as autumn tones of meadowed hills
it will have to be a dance down beside the water
where alder leaves are wending, and the wind has stilled.

She'd effect no costume, since eyes of river stone
are clean and gray. No prop either
for sky holds nothing once calling geese have flown.

Early evening of appointed day, descend toward river
downslope through cricket song, through browns
and hints of red, down to dimming water's shiver.

Where at last she'd dance—dance and twilight dance
till night's curtain falls
and hushes her into its expanse.

Solitude

Made camp among cedar and ponderosa. Rained only once
though moon went from half to full to half again.

One night that changing moon woke me
as though its light were swimming upstream in my chest.

One night that changing moon walked me naked to river
to pebble shore. One night found canoe

sculpted of nothing but fragrance and curve of shadow.
One night got in, pushed off, lay down. Floated.

Floated and floated. One night a rope in bow, a rope in stern
the canoe hung like hammock from Milky Way

and one night overhead keeping pace was bear
thick legs sloshing through stars. One night

a paw comes down, flips me onto earth.
When I raise head, I see cedar, ponderosa

hear river close at hand. Jumping in, the clean teeth
close swift all around. But now moonlight is swimming again

upriver in my chest, and the bear...the bear...the bear...
swims along too.

Surrender

More to mountain than mass, more to sky than space.

Hold out cupped hands and count
how many grains of chance it takes to fill them.

These trails through trees, mostly four legs walk.

Sometimes the wings of raven are black, sometimes silver
sometimes they are perfect and carry both mountain and moon.

I think I will leave today. When spring has melted
most the snow I might return. It all depends

on what fortune awaits this falling
into the cupped hands of the world.

Not One, Not Two

Morning sun in oak trees
the leaves are lit, and the world
is a child's face at story time.

Nothing to attain.
Summer will pass, winter come.
The tale goes on and on
no beginning, no end
no good part, no bad part

just a voice clear as the river
and paired with it, a listening
made of the same water.

Vigil for Release

Seat small as toad takes
silken night airs of river.

Something must let go
chest feather of passing bird
lilting its way down.

Must let go, must give in
to size of shadows
to grass stalks
crumbling slopes of rock

the way the whole sky
in deepening twilight
yields to the first star.

Everything Happens of Itself

Last night's thundercloud
woke me with its lightning.

Strung sheltering tarp as first drops fell.
Slept more I think, though maybe

boulders are awake
beneath their sheen of wet.

This morning: all clear.
Now top edge of sun peaks the ridge.

So perfect, the pale green of sagebrush
summoned out of light and leaf

as though there could be severance
between the seer and the seen.

To Actaeon

Sometimes you slip through veils without trying
wandering in wet forest this way and that
through clump of brush, cluster of small tree
following no sign just damp leaves
that idly make a silent path.

This maze-like motion goes down, levels
till pond opens unexpected like cavern chamber.

Through sheath of faint cover
wisps of willow, just budding
you see log bleached against dark water
turtles stretched out in secret leisure
sequestered world of water, weeds, sun on back.

And there, tall amongst turtles
perches a merganser— bright-lit, self-absorbed
preening brilliant white chest
dipping red bill again and again
and coming up rust head aflame
tufts ruffled and lifted like teased hair
like thundercloud, like beauty so condensed
it can only explode.

Touching the Untouchable

Once in a morning
under trees indistinguishable from time
I let the fingers of my being
find their way into shadow
where the cool of night still lay
like water without wet
clear and depthless
continuous with all other nights
all other waters.

A shaker jar full
and even by day, the stars tumbled out.
You told me then you could read
the constellations, the shapes of animals
the lyric stories forming out of dark.

I lay there, floating
with solid sense under back
while through tree tops
we could see the blue of sky
the moving clouds
we can see the world is dreaming
we can leave me here
drifting under trees.

tangled

art

of

aspen

leaf

with

wind

I love the handful of earth that you are.
Because of its meadows, vast as a planet,
I have no other star. You are my replica
of the multiplying universe.

—PABLO NERUDA

...bodily sex prepares you to make love as each moment's passion—
open, want-free oneness playing as desire-driven multiplicity.
Just as the sky can't be separated from its blue appearance,
yet is not itself blue, openness can't be other than
passionate happening, yet is not itself happening.

—DAVID DEIDA

Big Sur

She wears jeans and halter-top
while lupines splash about her calves like lake water.
Not much else to do but follow.

Last night she was moonlight filtered through ferns
a blanket of fur rippling with hillside air.
She was the breathing of farthest trees
as they opened coastal body
to near-most murmur of tide and stars.

Now she walks far above the sea
while grass and flowered meadow
cascade down, cascade down
to soundless white of surf.

Not much else to do but follow
as whales do shoreline, hawks contours of space.
Jeans and halter-top— she saunters easy
as though she weren't continent's westward prow
plunging me headlong into blue water, blue wind.

Moon and Mountains

She reads lying belly down in summer grass
propped on elbows, facing away.

Now and then naked legs crisscross in air
while I survey contours she cannot see.

Beyond this glade are granite geographies
curvesome mile of slope and ridgeline vantage.

But I might till nightfall just linger here
when moon will roll over mountain ridge

to incite and silhouette on wall of tent
a tangled art of aspen leaf and wind.

Biblical Study

There is moment
most timely

we seem
to mutually sense

when chest and hip
make move from prelude

and braced above
by arm by knee

align and settle
into something

the ancients
aptly named

as knowing.

Earth and Sky

If you are leaves then I am rain—
you greet foremost my fall to earth
and I bring you the cool scents of heaven.

Or let's call you rain and me leaves.
Either way the sound the forest makes is us—
that leaping of every lobe of leaf
that shattering of firmament's every pebble.

You are rooted, I am sky-born.
You my canopy of rapture, my bed of dissolution.
Or let's make me the foliage of your freedom
and you the glistening weight that bows me earthward.

Either way, there are trees, there are clouds
there are you and I, leaves and lips—
either way we will body tonight
a downpour of soaking presence
an uproar thirsty with devotion.

Flamenco Night

Love is an island between dreamy and alert.
Love is a castaway clutching a relic of home.
Love is driftwood under the palest of stars
suffused with the float of no end to how far.

.   .   .

Dinner first, the table in the corner.
Red wine, Flamenco music
napkins still docile in laps.

Copper hoop earrings, and a flush
of melancholy, because the ocean
soughs so near and anything can drown.

Warm bread, more wine
clams in broth of butter and garlic.

And then suddenly
the ocean sends a surge of dancers to shore.
They tangle in the seaweed of her hair
leap from leg of lamb, seize torches
ignite a bonfire on rocky headland
and he's the naked whirling captain
in tempestuous sea of those sparks.

Dessert brings a drifting fog
that cools meadow grasses.
Rounded swells smooth the car ride home.

Opossum in road. Paused headlights
show it listing like ship going down
hiss faint as surf at distance.
That's right she says, take it to side shadows
lay it in harbor of trees
panting like back and forth sway of buoys.

The ocean is their bed, and he's never
been so in love with salt, how it
sings to horizon, never so in love with tides
or how heron atop billows of kelp
calls wingspread out of waves, never
so in love with phosphorescence
how it lights with a push, then quells
leaving sea at last to its moan of darkness.

          ·   ·   ·

And love is an island between dreamy and alert.
Love is a castaway clutching a relic of home.
Love is driftwood under the palest of stars
suffused with the float of no end to how far.

chipped

as

mottled

sky

———————

...the swallows grew still and bats came out light as breath
around the stranger by himself in the echoes
what did I have to do with anything I could remember
all I did not know went on beginning around me....

— W.S. MERWIN

Like vanishing dew,
a passing apparition
or the sudden flash
of lightning— already gone–
thus should one regard oneself.

–IKKYU

As Above, So Below

The song the sea washed up was so unequivocal
that crows who dipped their bills
would later rain it from their wings.

And so the message was carried
from headland to headland, till night's horizon
caught and cast it into waves that break
with no sound of surf on shore.

Lost after that. The voice of crows harsh again.
Two sentinels were posted—
one to gaze on stars for source of glimmer

one to be the life of sand
that finds its breath on the bottom of the sea.

Metamorphosis

Three days offshore it bobbed
lifting into sight on swells, hidden in troughs.
Seals paid no mind, nor pelicans
in wave-skimming flights.

Breezes played in alders, and he knew by them
when the pattern shifted.
With stars and river near at hand
he sat through night, sound of surf

like fingers lifting root hairs from scalp.
At dawn he walked to beach, saw deer tracks
circling what had washed in.
Wet drapes of seaweed still clung.

In weeks that followed he did nothing different.
One afternoon swallows busy above river
he felt something settle weightless
into what he could no longer call himself.

Findings in the Desert

A burro's bone and the sprawled decay
of a miner's shack. Wind

going nowhere but into itself
and behind it, stillness—

a mountain lifted away.

And I wonder about the texture
of a tenderness barely touched

how it breathes like sun-burnt stone
submerged in weightless water

blooms one night
then perishes for a thousand.

Beneficence

Sun a low slant
and distance curves back into itself

like finding in fallen leaves
an amulet chipped as mottled sky.

Maybe the old man
will open his door now

tell story at last
his voice a crawl through aspen grove

not even knowing
one's back has become weighted with gold.

Dissolution

At daybreak in desert
two ravens on rock
moon still up in west.

Hills wrinkle deep with shadow.
When the birds fly off
no one stays behind.

Rumination in the Desert

Nothing to do this morning but live the light
that passes through leaves of last year
their edges lit as eyelids

like yours in sleep, bright perhaps
with dream behind them, of cottonwoods
say, just before start of green journey.

And how bird song is also a light
flickering over backdrop of silence.

Even memory of you with sleeping eyelids
is light-flash flaring across dimensionless dark.

And so the world falls into absence and presence
like what our eyes will see
when next they open upon each other

that moment alive like all moments
a petal buoyed up by darkness
that allows us to love light.

last

utterance

of the

maples

I do not know which to prefer,

The beauty of inflections

Or the beauty of innuendoes,

The blackbird whistling

Or just after.

— *WALLACE STEVENS*

Nobody likes to die

But an old man

Can know

A kind of gratefulness

Toward time that kills him,

Everything he loved was made of it.

—*GALWAY KINNELL*

Not the Tao That Can Be Spoken

I could not tell the legs of heron as it flew
in the volumeless space we know as August
where to land next, where in the world
one can alight with that last braking sweep
we know as feather, blue and gray
above the wide river corridor of cobbles.

Those cobbles, so stark and singular
that do not tell their names even to each other.
No-name is the river that hides its body
as a whisper filtering through summer gravels
and sunlight gleams on the bleached arm of an old snag
that points like sundial to the no-time
that is not burning in the burning of the sun.

I could not say what the forest was in its silence
in its old standing, what the beings were
that flashed their rhythms of wing-light
before their merge into mountain shadow.

To the dry terraces of stone and grass, I could not tell
what rain is, what snow, what no-word
does with wind, with clouds that are wind's face
with faces that are earth's clouds
with what we know as earth and all its faces
whirled by what must be wind's wind.

After WS Merwin

If this were the last day of the world

I would want it October
earth wet with recent rains

the leaves a yellow of prophesy
that speaks with no need of tomorrow

that last utterance of the maples
as the stream still comes down off the mountain

and the mountain still falls forward
into its own falling. The last of the world

and nothing has changed—
mountains and waters, and the trees

letting all go, as they do their leaves
still shining with the last touch of rain.

Each Small Bead

With each good rain, the streams of the heart
begin their song again, begin their tumble down the mountain
legs of young deer, green meadows of play.

Sky is colorless in good rain
an ocean that might float the earth
as bauble of driftwood, endless cradle in roll of waves.

A stone hut shingled in cedar
takes on a sheen in rain
as though polished by one who never lives or dies

who walks behind the farthest curtain of rain
behind whatever story we have
for cloud and mountain, for aspen leaves falling

when the gold of the world
lights on our skin at sunrise and again at sunset.
We were wandering once

we knew the rains, we knew the winds
we knew how to walk with affection and daring.
Inside caves were deep wells

and children tossed pebbles that fell and fell
and some heard at last a splash and some didn't
and those that heard

said it was two impossibilities meeting
two eternities, two hearts colliding at a mirror
and reflecting into each other

such that neither reached bottom.
Someone is sitting at the doorway of the hut
and one wind says he is facing out and another wind

says she is facing in, and all the while the good rain falls
and each small bead bounces and coheres
with a being every bit as buoyant as the earth.

After Wallace Stevens

I placed a jar in California
and clear it was upon a hill.
Earth shone right through
and sky was water to fill.

The mountain rose above—
source no art can tame.
The jar was small upon the ground
to which it yielded all acclaim.

No dominion anywhere.
All jars are empty and bare.
Like bird, like bush
they sprout everywhere.

Long Ago and Still to Come

Once, when morning sun first hit the river
we saw the glinting of a bird beyond first trees
a glinting of silver it seemed, though some thought gold
and one heard a call that was bell-like, she said

but a small bell, not made of metal, ceramic maybe
and old, as though carried by boat across sea.
We went toward the call, wading through push
of thigh-high water and found a silence

behind the trees that was also old
and smelled of cedar chests and letters long since forgotten.
No one saw the bird, but a single feather was found
and brought back to camp. We sang that night

around the fire, and someone told a dream in morning
of a bird that could dive beneath the river
and come up, one turn of the moon later
at ease in the middle of the ocean.

One Glory

All afternoon—turbulence of cloud
a gradual graying and amassing
thunder in various quarters
and wind, gusting through cottonwoods
harries yellow leaves across river gravel.

This drama never ends. An old man
says that once in summer river
he saw her naked— half in, half out.
That seeing was enough.
One glory, at least, to carry to his grave.

Floods have roiled passions down the river
tumbling boulders, ripping roots from banks.
More often, the quiet times—
baby mergansers single file trailing their mother
across alder-lined and swallow-dipped pools.

It never ends.
Children, hands outstretched
chase darting color of falling leaves.
The man grows dizzy, wakes far downriver
the sound of breaking surf a surprise.

Could it be, he wonders
that the cryptic call of his life
had swum upstream to meet him
had hatched from a pearly roundness
rolling on the cradle of ocean floor.

Ars Poetica

"...the dream of every poem {is} to be a myth."
−GALLWAY KINNELL

1.

This night, this very night
airborne and erratic
a thousand arousings
beat on the sinewy stretched
membranes of their wings
archaic and inaccessible
crowding oak-leaf shadow
spilling from sparse silhouette of pine.

The night is deluged
with inaudible callings
unanswerable motions.
In such water as this
the trout open-mouthed
stupors in the deepest pool
the eel adheres to its single rock
while overhead the current
fragrant and haunting
sweeps torrentially by.

2.

Just out of touch, just off shore
poems press south with drive of hidden tails.

The great arcs of their rolling backs
but hint of the muscled bulk surging below

and the white blasts of their breathing
are brief ghosts collapsing down to blue.

Only the furthest reach of wave sloshes my feet.
while the primordial water heaves out there—
endless, elusive, and enticingly replete.

3.

If it were critiqued
that all my poetry
amounted to variations of
I was here

acquiescence
would be immediate
if allowed to add
You were too.

4.

If I sing of green, if I sing of blue
if of life and word
I make a springtime melody

look a layer under
look some years ahead

every poem I write, every gesture
lays its heart
upon the growing ground of elegy.

Boundless

One day he stepped off trail
and he stepped off what wasn't trail
and then he stepped off that
till he was in a place
that could have been all places
though he recognized it
as the one place he had always been.

Sunlight lit the maple leaves
to a green that washed him
and the sound of stream was moth-like
in its flight right through him.

He found a pebble
whose weight in palm was endless—
a galaxy dropping down into something
that loved being both a darkness
as well as the whisper stars make
in the windless world of their own falling.

A black phoebe flew from perch
grabbed insect out of air
and when it returned
he felt the grip of slender toes
the balance of body
as days pass over slopes of grassland and oak

and he was inside a story
that had little to do with him
and yet its edges
were as close to him
as its center.

addendum

Poetry, Qigong,
and Expansive States of Being

UNLIKE PAINTING, SCULPTURE, OR INSTRUMENTAL MUSIC, POETRY is clearly a verbal art. But the appeal of poetry through the ages is exactly because, even in its use of words, it can nevertheless be a portal for the reader (or listener) into a moment not limited by language. And an expansive moment, however achieved, has proven itself deeply appealing to humans. Not to equate them, but music, dance, ritual, drugs, alcohol, meditation, and qigong are all popular and effective means of altering our consciousness, and their history of use goes back to the very beginnings of human culture.

The tightest space an individual can occupy is not a prison cell but a verbally compulsive mind. Insanity, as we recognize it, is often exactly that: a person unable to get any distance from the relentless influx of thoughts, feelings, images, all of which present so often as "voices". Or in the case of severe anxiety, the suffering individual is listening to a constant repetitive litany of internally voiced fears. Then we come to the so-called "normal neurosis" of the average person (in contemporary non-indigenous cultures, at least). Even this fully functional person suffers from confinement in the egoic mind, commonly referred to as "internal chatter", the voice-like mental process that works diligently to identify, categorize, qualify, and manage everything that the self perceives in its version of reality.

An assumption in this brief essay is that the reader is aware of their occasional (or predominant) entrapment in the tight space of the small self. It has been said that the spiritual path can only begin when the individual experiences very clearly that it is their own mental and emotional processes that are limiting them to an unsatisfactory or disappointing existence. With that realization, the enemy is understood to be us, and an internal path toward some level of liberation can then be chosen. Besides spiritual practice, art, exercise, and nature, to name a few, also offer common avenues out of the confinement.

Emerson refers to poets as "liberating gods". He says, "They are free, and they make free." The creative act of writing is clearly an altered state. One must allow the subconscious to come forth. The blank page is emblematic of the blank mind, the open mind, the inscrutable darkness from which the sudden flash of words appear. Ironically perhaps, the poet is someone who is able to leave the verbal mind, and enter a space that is in itself wordless and yet out of which words cohere.

Gary Snyder has defined poetry as "the skilled and inspired use of the voice and language to embody rare and powerful states of mind that are in immediate origin personal to the singer, but at deeper levels common to all who listen."

To link Emerson and Snyder, we may come to the understanding that a poet is free to the extent that they are able to enter more-than-verbal, non-egoic moments. In a poet's additional ability to simultaneously, or subsequently, find verbal expression of those moments, their poems seem capable of encoding and transmitting a parallel liberating experience to the reader.

This dual aspect of poetry almost certainly goes back to shamanism. The shaman, through whatever means or circumstance (prayer, fasting, dance, physical ordeal, plant psychedelics, illness, etc.) would come to embody a rare and powerful state of mind, and would then often return to ordinary consciousness with a song (poem). That song would have the capacity to carry the shaman back into the altered state when needed, and it would often also have a powerful effect on the listener, if used for example in a healing ritual. Traditional notions of a "spell" or "charm" come to mind in this context.

Walt Whitman read Emerson's essays very closely and had certainly heard the phrase "liberating gods". It may be fair to say that he passionately wanted to fulfill that archetypal role of the poet. In his "Song Of Myself", he openly declares: "Stop this day and night with me and you shall possess the origin of all poems...." I personally think he accomplished that grand ambition about as well as can be hoped for in the medium of poetry. One could contemplate and write at great length as to what it means to "possess the origin of all poems", but to keep it very simple and generalized here, we might say that Whitman is pointing toward an ability to touch into creativity itself. This mysterious source, this infinite potentiality seems to secret itself in the subconscious processes of the individual, but it has analogous echoes in the larger cosmic and evolutionary processes from which spring all manifestations of matter, life, and mind.

Not all poetry is, or need be, as shamanic, as mystical, as Whitman's. In fact, in the contemporary literary scene, it would probably be considered inappropriate, even pretentious, to undertake something beyond one's own small sphere of time, place, culture, social status, gender, etc. and hypothesize a more universal relevance.

I'm going to leave that post-modern critique aside, and return to the notion of the more-than-verbal moment, and its apparent appeal to many people in many cultures and time periods. It is beyond the small scope of this essay to attempt to say more precisely how poetry can have its liberating effects. A baby spider will throw out a thread to be caught and carried away by wind. New studies apparently show that there are electrostatic forces involved in the initial lift off, not just up-draft breeze. But the young spider has no conceptual understanding of gravity, the repellency of opposite electrical charges, or wind speed. The spider simply climbs a grass stalk, releases a thread, and away it goes.

Poetry may make spiders of us all. We know it works, that it can have a transportive effect, but we can't exactly explain why or how. Somehow the poem's elements of sound, rhythm, image, inflection, metaphor, etc. all work in synergy with a human nervous system of brain waves, neurotransmitters, endorphins, and hormones to create moments which can lift us away from our self-absorbed concerns and our cognitive confines. Poetry can carry us into a more expanded realm of beauty, insight, awareness, understanding, and can fling us far and wide in the vast all-directional space of emotion and feeling.

In this current volume, and in the previous, I share my poems as a possible means for others to experience an expanded moment. The writing of them has already liberated me into such a moment, and hopefully that mysterious lift echoes and reverberates still within the space that is the poem, though each reader, like each spider, will have their own trajectory through it.

In my love for more-than-verbal moments, I want to briefly share another method that I have found effective in shifting me away from the small self. Qigong, like poetry, can be a liberating god.

As mentioned earlier, it is only a specific and limited part of the mind that lives in the world of words. The body (and large portions of the mind) do not inhabit that world. They live elsewhere, in a realm more interconnected, and thus less isolated, less dualistic, than the talking head of the ego. I believe poetry, both in its creation and in its reading, is best practiced as a somatic experience, though it is easy in our culture to let poetry's participation in the cerebral world of words be primary and exclusive.

Qigong, on the other hand, involves full participation in breathing, standing still, and moving slowly, thus its somatic orientation is immediate. To the degree that we can be fully present in and as our body is the degree to which we have moved away from the internal chatter of the egoic self. To practice qigong (and other somatic arts), one needs the willingness to leave that verbal self-referential world and not panic. The vigilant ego, that wants to control, manage, label, and judge everything that is happening, clings to itself as to a life raft. And yet polar to that impulse is the one desirous to let go of the raft, to be liberated from confinement, to cross a threshold into the pleasures and virtues of the more expansive moment.

Qigong can get us over that threshold. I am going to present here some very basic guidance in standing qigong meditation. My teacher in qigong and Taoism/Buddhism is Roshi Teja Bell (qigongdharma.com). Though Roshi Bell has never explicitly said "stop this day and night with me and you shall possess the origin of all poems", I do feel that in the theory and manner of his teaching, he presents the invitation for qigong to be a pathway into the relaxed space of potentiality: the darkness, the stillness, the unmoving turbulence from which all creativity can emerge. In the Chinese language of qigong, this unmanifest space is known as wuji. It's the origin of all movements, all poems.

If I wanted to find one sentence that gave the simplest but most comprehensive overview of how to practice qigong, I would choose a line from Mary Oliver's poetry: "You only have to let the soft animal of your body love what it loves".

To be an animal is to be natural. Can we embrace the animal nature of ourselves and just stand in the present moment, loosely, softly, naturally? Can we let a bodily feeling of love and welcome radiate outward from us as source (centrifugal), while also allowing the feel of love and welcome to radiate inward to us (centripetal)?

I present this practice as an exploration, a playful engagement within the vast range of attention/consciousness/awareness/expansion that is possible to us. Even a 1-minute practice can be rich, and extending it up to 15 or 20 minutes (like a modest sitting meditation session) can also be rich. Below, I will give my briefest possible overall guidelines for all standing meditation (beyond Mary Oliver's superior brevity!), and then I will follow it up with two particular more specific approaches for individual sessions. Though the primary practice in standing meditation, as in sitting meditation, is just to be there without any agenda, sometimes it can be engaging to provide slightly more direction to ourselves. Again, these are best undertaken not as discipline but as rest, reprieve, nourishment, play. Feeling (somatic, energetic, and heart) rather than thought, is the guide.

Guidelines for undirected standing qigong meditation:
+ Preferably outside, but indoors will work, too.
+ Imagine a lift from the very top of the head, as though suspended. Chin will tuck down and in slightly to straighten back of neck. (This is the influence of "Heaven", in Taoist terminology)

- Feel the bottom of the feet. Now really feel the bottom of the feet. Now really, really feel the bottom of the feet. (This is the influence of "Earth", in Taoist terminology)

- Let knees soften and bend slightly to allow tailbone to drop (which may feel like a slight tuck forward of lower spine).

- Hips rest exactly above feet, chest exactly above hips, head exactly above chest.

- Eyes in soft gaze, allowing full peripheral vision.

- Relax. Let the soft animal of your body love what it loves.

For the two directed practices that follow, begin with the general guidelines above, then move into the additional suggestions below. These are awareness games. (Besides Roshi Teja Bell as primary, I have been influenced by Brian O'Connor *Awareness Games* and Lock Kelley *The Way of Effortless Mindfulness*). Much as poetry uses words to incite a more-than-verbal moment, these meditations use words to perhaps stimulate an expansion into the wordless empty vastness of embodied awareness.

I. Free Fall

- We are falling.

- If earth or floor were to drop away, we'd fall instantly.

- Feel the bottom of the feet; that feeling

- Is the falling

- Feel the bottom of the feet; that feeling

- Is the rising

- Simultaneously and equal, there is falling, there is rising.

- Taoists might say, that along with all other beings, we stand poised and balanced equally between Heaven and Earth.

- Imagine intellectual amnesia. You forget all common sense assumptions of gravity. Stop explaining. Let the body feel. Not the mind, scanning and surveying the body. Not the mind, doing mindfulness. But the body of energy and awareness being itself.

- Be Being itself.

II. Neutrinos

- Cosmic particles so small, they rarely interact with matter.

- As a spaceship might pass through the vastness of space, with light years of distance between stars, so neutrinos pass right through our bodies all the time.

- To them, and to physics, we are much more space than solid.

- Stand still, and imagine neutrinos from all angles journeying unimpeded right through you.

- Feel space outside no different than space inside.

- Be the space/time that does not move or alter even as neutrinos speed through.

I find that standing meditation done outside intrinsically carries similarities to the Buddha's sitting meditation posture with the Bhumisparsha mudra, in which his right hand reaches down to touch the earth, said to be calling the earth goddess, Sthavara, to bear witness to his enlightenment. In the standing posture as opposed to sitting, it seems less easy to get lost in daydreaming or abstraction, enabling the embodied reality of the present moment on earth to suffuse and ground the meditation.

Sometimes after I stand, I'll turn to the blank page to see if any words want to precipitate out of the amorphous cloud of possibility, but more often than not, I'll just wander off with the sense that earth, life, love, and their beauty are already poetry enough.

acknowledgments

"Dissolution" (with a different title) has appeared online in
The Plum Tree Tavern. (https://theplumtreetavern.blogspot.
com/search?q=abel)

"Known and Unknown" and "Desert Shade" have appeared
in *The Wayfarer*. Winter, 2021.

"Solitude", "Metamorphosis", and "Deer Hoof" appeared in
slightly different version in *Nostos*, fall 2021.

Thanks to Charlotte Pence, David Rigsbee, and Amelia
Martens, all who read versions of some of these poems and
offered helpful feedback.

Many thanks to Leslie Browning, founder and editor of Homebound
Publications, for the great gift and affirmation of seeing value in my
art and bringing it carefully to print. And thanks also for the other
authors she publishes, and the ever-expanding pool of wonderful and
worthwhile writing that she has helped shepherd into the world.

My wife Willow, besides being a teacher to me, as expressed in the
dedication, of the sensibilities that lead to art, has also somehow
managed to combine in her person without conflict the mysterious
potency of Muse and the very practical function of well-tuned editor.

about the author

Walker Abel has published four volumes of poetry, all with Homebound Publications. His poems spring from the two fundamental influences of his adult life: decades of intimacy with wilderness areas of the West, and decades of engagement with the practices and teachings within Taoism and Zen Buddhism. For 27 years, Walker taught environmental studies field programs in the University of California system. These 9-week classes were conducted entirely off-campus on a series of backpacking trips. As an ecopsychologist, Walker loved watching students open to the transformative effect of extended nature immersion, as he also loved experiencing those effects inside himself. Walker is currently a student of Roshi Teja Bell, who blends Taoism and Buddhism into an embodied synthesis (qigongdharma.com).

HOMEBOUND
PUBLICATIONS

Since 2011 We are an award-winning independent publisher striving to ensure that the mainstream is not the only stream. More than a company, we are a community of writers and readers exploring the larger questions we face as a global village. It is our intention to preserve contemplative storytelling. We publish full-length introspective works of creative non-fiction, literary fiction, and poetry.

Look for Our Imprints Little Bound Books, Owl House Books, The Wayfarer Magazine, Wayfarer Books & Navigator Graphics

WWW.HOMEBOUNDPUBLICATIONS.COM

WAYFARER

BASED IN THE BERKSHIRE MOUNTAINS, MASS.

The Wayfarer Magazine. Since 2012, The Wayfarer has been offering literature, interviews, and art with the intention to inspires our readers, enrich their lives, and highlight the power for agency and change-making that each individual holds. By our definition, a wayfarer is one whose inner-compass is ever-oriented to truth, wisdom, healing, and beauty in their own wandering. The Wayfarer's mission as a publication is to foster a community of contemplative voices and provide readers with resources and perspectives that support them in their own journey.

Wayfarer Books is our newest imprint! After nearly 10 years in print, *The Wayfarer Magazine* is branching out from our magazine to become a full-fledged publishing house offering full-length works of eco-literature!

Wayfarer Farm & Retreat is our latest endeavor, springing up the Berkshire Mountains of Massachusetts. Set to open to the public in 2024, the 15 acre retreat will offer workshops, farm-to-table dinners, off-grid retreat cabins, and artist residencies.

WWW.WAYFARERBOOKS.ORG

9 781956 368116